CONTENTS

COMMUNIST THEORY

The Communist Party Manifesto was written by Karl Marx and Friedrich Engels and first published in **1848** in German.

The manifesto argued that **capitalism was making the working class poorer.** Inevitably the workers would revolt and this would lead to the "violent overthrow of the bourgeoisie".

The resulting state or government would be "the proletariat organised as the ruling class". **The state would take all capital, economic production and property from the bourgeoisie.**

After this, there would be no more "class antagonisms" because there would be no more classes.

Communism:

A little book
of facts

"
THE
THEORY OF
THE COMMUNISTS
MAY BE SUMMED
UP IN THE SINGLE
SENTENCE:
ABOLITION
OF PRIVATE
PROPERTY

" Communist Party
Manifesto

Karl Marx and Friedrich Engels.

66

WE SHALL HAVE AN ASSOCIATION, IN WHICH THE FREE DEVELOPMENT OF EACH IS THE FREE DEVELOPMENT OF ALL.

99

ESTABLISHMENT OF COMMUNIST REGIMES

1917 Russian revolution led by Vladimir Lenin, leading to the creation of "the Soviet Union".
1921 Mongolian revolution.
1939 Eastern Poland. Invaded by the Soviet Union.
1939 Estonia, Lithuania and Latvia. Obliged by threat of force to agree to Soviet take-over.
1940 Finnish Karelia. Invaded by the Soviet Union.
1944 Estonia, Lithuania and Latvia. Retaken from Germany by the Soviet Union.
1944 Poland. Retaken from Germany by the Soviet Uni◀
1944 Romania. Soviet occupation followed by a rigged election.
1944 Bulgaria. Occupied by the Soviet Union.
1944 Albania. Italian occupiers were expelled. Achieved power through assassination and election fraud.
1945 East Germany. Occupied by the Soviet Union.
1945 Yugoslavia. Achieved power through the defeat of Germany and winning civil conflict. Led by Josip Tito.
1945 North Korea. Allocated to the Soviet Union after surrender of Japan in Second World War.
1948 Czechoslovakia. Soviet-backed coup d'état.
1948 Hungary. Communist Party backed by the Soviet Union gained power by terror and election fraud.

HITLER GREETING STALIN AFTER THEY HAD **BOTH** INVADED POLAND, DIVIDING IT BETWEEN THEM.

1945-54 North Vietnam Communist Party led by Ho Chi Minh overcame rivals and French colonial power.

1949 China. Achieved power after Japanese defeat and civil war. Led by Mao Zedong.

1959 Cuba. Revolution led by Fidel Castro.

1969 Somalia. Military coup.

1974 Ethiopia. Military coup developed into Communism by 1979.

1975 South Vietnam. Invasion by North Vietnamese Communist forces.

1975 Laos. Vietnam-backed coup.

1975 Cambodia. Civil war won by China-backed Khmer Rouge. Led by Pol Pot.

1978 Afghanistan. Coup.

Other **African and South American** countries were influenced by Communism for longer or shorter periods without adhering fully to Communist ideology.

The Soviet Union included countries which had been part of the Russian Empire including **Ukraine, Georgia, Belarus and Kazakhstan.**

In none of the 23 countries above was the take-over of power achieved by a free, democratic vote.

A free press, if it existed before, was shut down in all these countries after a Communist take-over.

The bodies of South Vietnamese soldiers along with several US advisers killed fighting the Viet Cong. Horst Faas/AP.

7

Factory workers assembling tanks at a Soviet plant in the Urals.

STATE TAKE-OVER
OF THE ECONOMY

INDUSTRIAL COMPANIES, BANKS AND OTHER BUSINESSES WERE TAKEN OVER BY THE GOVERNMENT.

Everything from tractors to drawing pins was made by state enterprises following orders and targets set by the government.

Private property was forcibly expropriated. Owners who objected were treated with various degrees of severity ranging up to and including being shot.

After the Russian Revolution, peasants and small farmers were required to sell part of their produce at below market prices to the state. They were sometimes reluctant to accept this. A shortfall of grain procured by the Soviet government in 1927 was blamed by Stalin on hoarding by "kulaks" – small-scale farmers. He accelerated a policy of "collectivisation" – forcing existing small farms and peasant holdings to combine into bigger farms run either by a "collective" of peasants or the state. Many kulaks and peasants resisted. Thousands were killed or deported to Siberia in eastern Russia.

Stalin thought collective farms, using modern methods, would dramatically increase production. Instead, grain production declined and contributed to a famine in 1932-33. Grain was also taken from farms by force and exported. The worst of this was imposed on Ukraine where **3.9 million** starved to death in an internationally recognised crime and tragedy known as "Holodomor".

Starved people on a street in Kharkiv, 1933.

COLLECTIVISATION OF FARMS

China (1958-62) and
Vietnam in (1958-
60) also imposed
collectivisation of
farms.
In both cases this also
led to famine. In China,
45 million died of
starvation according to
one of the more recent
estimates.

ONE-PARTY STATES

Some Communists, including Lenin, depicted themselves as democrats. But after the revolution, Russia had an election in which Lenin's party, the Bolsheviks, received only **24%** of the vote. The resulting assembly sat for one day and rejected a Bolshevik proposal. That night, Lenin, who had control of troops, had the doors closed and locked. He declared that the assembly was dissolved. It did not sit again.

In all the Communist countries, one-party states were established and those who opposed them were imprisoned or worse. In some places, such as East Germany, other parties were allowed to exist **but not to have power.**

NEWSPAPERS
~~AND MAGAZINES~~
~~WHICH OPPOSED~~
~~COMMUNIST~~
~~GOVERNMENTS~~
~~WERE CLOSED.~~

REIGNS OF
TERROR AND PURGES

In 1918-22, many opponents of the Communist regime in Russia, property owners and kulaks were executed. For example, in August 1918, Lenin gave this order following a revolt in Penza region,

> **HANG (ABSOLUTELY HANG, IN FULL VIEW OF THE PEOPLE) NO FEWER THAN ONE HUNDRED KNOWN KULAKS, FILTHY RICH MEN, BLOODSUCKERS.**

A total of **8,000** executions took place during August to November 1918 alone. This pattern was repeated in many Communist countries.

In the Great Terror (1936-38) initiated by Stalin, **680,000 to 1 million** people were killed in the Soviet Union many of whom were party members. In this way, Stalin quashed opposition from within the party as well as from outside.

Mao Zedong in China conducted purges of members of his own party both before and after he achieved power. In the "Cultural Revolution" (1966-76), an estimated **750,000 to 2 million** died, many of whom were Communist Party members.

Secret police spied on people to check if they were disloyal to the regime. People were expected to inform on each other. This was organised to a high degree by the Stasi secret police in East Germany.

TORTURE WAS ROUTINELY USED AS PUNISHMENT AND TO EXTRACT CONFESSIONS OF GUILT IN THE MAJORITY OF COMMUNIST REGIMES AND PERHAPS IN ALL OF THEM.

DEPORTATIONS —
6.3 MILLION PEOPLE

1930-31 **1.8 million** kulaks were forcibly taken from their homes in the Soviet Union and moved to remote parts of the country such as Siberia.

1932-39 A further **1 million** peasants and ethnic minorities were similarly deported.

1940-52 Another **3.5 million** ethnic minorities were deported.

The deportations between **1940** and **1952** include ones from countries taken over by the Soviet Union such as the Baltic states: Latvia, Estonia, Lithuania. For example, **130,000** people including women and children were deported from Lithuania alone. These were in addition to the **150,000** people sent to Gulag camps.

People were often given very little time, such as an hour to gather some belongings to take with them. Many were put into cattle wagons on trains and travelled for days. Some died from cold, hunger and exhaustion

THE GULAG AND "RE-EDUCATION CAMPS"

Work camps and prisons were extensively used to maintain the power of Communist parties. Opponents of the regimes and those suspected of being opponents were sent there. Wives of opponents were sent to them in the Soviet Union even if they had themselves done nothing.

The work camp system was known as the GULAG in the Soviet Union, an acronym in Russian for Chief Administration of Corrective Labour Camps. It is estimated that **18 million** people were consigned to GULAG camps between 1930 and 1953 of whom **1.5 to 1.7 million** died, mostly because of cold, hunger and lack of medical treatment.

China also had forced labour penal camps called Laogai (up until 1994). Estimates of the deaths in the harsh conditions vary between **15 and 27 million.** Communist indoctrination sessions were compulsory.

In Vietnam, hundreds of thousands of former members of the South Vietnamese army were told they would spend two weeks or a month in "Re-education Camps". This was a trick. Many were kept for seven years or more in harsh conditions which included punishment by being held in metal boxes which became extremely hot in the tropical climate.

Workers on oil drilling exploration in USSR, 1968.

ACHIEVEMENTS

Rapid industrialisation. Steel production was considered a measure of industrial might and Stalin wanted a big increase. Accordingly output of steel rose fourfold between 1928 (4.3 million tons) and 1937 (17.7million). However, this period includes the widespread famine of 1932/3. Other countries had earlier periods of industrialisation without mass starvation.

The Soviet Union had a major role in the defeat of Germany in the Second World War. However, the only reason the Soviet Union fought Germany was that Germany attacked it. Moreover the Soviet Union then took advantage of its military strength to subjugate Poland, East Germany, Hungary, Czechoslovakia, Lithuania, Estonia and Latvia.

Improvement in the position of women. Legal equality was quickly established in the Soviet Union and women were encouraged to take on industrial and other jobs. But similar legal changes took place in many other countries in the 20th century.

DEATH TOLL OF COMMUNIST REGIMES

Eastern Europe	Afghanistan	Cambodia	North Korea	Soviet Union	China
1 million	**1.5** million	**2** million	**2** million	**20** million	**65** million

Over **90** million in total

The highest death toll per capita was in Cambodia. Estimates vary but about **2 million** were killed out of a population of 7.3 million – more than a quarter. Prisoners were taken to the so-called Killing Fields, where they were executed, often with pickaxes, to save bullets.

The figures above include deaths by execution, torture, man-made famine and harsh conditions during deportation, forced labour and imprisonment. They do not include deaths in civil wars of which there were many.

Stacked human skulls at the Killing Fields of Choeung Ek, Cambodia

Source: The Black Book of Communism (p4).
There are different ways of calculating death tolls
and the availability of reliable records varies from one
country to another. Therefore estimates can vary
considerably.

ECONOMIC PERFORMANCE

Communist countries		Non-Communist countries	
East Germany	$9,679	USA	$21,082
Soviet Union	$9,210	Japan	$15,600
Hungary	$6,108	West Germany	$15,300
Poland	$4,565	France	$14,600
China	$370	United Kingdom	$14,300

Estimated GDP per capita 1990.

	East Germany	West Germany
Computer ownership	12%	37%
Telephone ownership	16%	99%
Wait for new car	10+ years	None

Western products ranging from confectionery
to cigarettes and cars could not be purchased
by ordinary people in Communist regimes.
Sometimes they could be bought in special
stores which only Communist officials could go to.

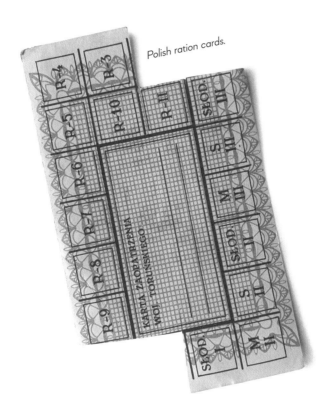

Polish ration cards.

FALL OF COMMUNIST STATES

1989

2nd May: **Hungarian** border guards began removing sections of the border fence with Austria.

4th June: Solidarity, a national trade union in **Poland,** won an overwhelming victory in a partially free election.

9th October: 70,000 demonstrated against **the East German** government in Leipzig. The police refused to fire on them.

9th November: **the Berlin Wall** fell.

1990

Poland, Hungary, East Germany and Czechoslovakia democratically and peacefully elected non-Communist governments. In **Bulgaria,** the Communist Party renounced Marxist Leninism, renamed itself the Bulgarian Socialist Party and was re-elected.

In **Romania,** the authorities shot at demonstrators but then the army changed sides. Elections were held. **Estonia, Latvia and Lithuania** declared their independence from the Soviet Union.

1991

December: **the Soviet Union** dissolved. Russia became the Russian Federation.

China and Vietnam are still ruled by the Communist Party but have given up pure Communism. Both allow private property and have stock markets.

Cuba is also still ruled by the Communist Party but it has gradually eased state ownership of the economy. Private sector employment almost tripled between 1981 and 2000 to 23 per cent.

North Korea is still ruled by the Communist Party but, in practice, it has become an hereditary, totalitarian dictatorship.

Chinese stock market quotes.

KARL MARX FORECAST THAT COMMUNIST REVOLUTIONS WOULD INEVITABLY TAKE PLACE IN THE MORE ADVANCED INDUSTRIALISED COUNTRIES.

Marx said it was inevitable under capitalism that the labouring classes would become poorer.

Marx forecast that the increasingly poor labouring classes would instigate revolutions.

Marx forecast that state control of the economy (Socialism) would inevitably give way to an ideal society in which no one needed or wanted to own property (Communism).

IN PRACTICE, NO COMMUNIST REVOLUTION HAS TAKEN PLACE IN ANY ADVANCED INDUSTRIAL COUNTRY.

In practice, under capitalism, the labouring classes have become a great deal richer. Real average wages in Britain have increased eight times since 1848 when the Communist manifesto was written.

In practice, the Communist take-overs of power have been led by intellectuals and others coming from the better off parts of society such as Lenin, Trotsky, Mao Zedong and Ho Chi Minh.

The ideal state which Marx forecast as inevitable has not taken place in any country.

> **We must not depict socialism as if socialists will bring it to us on a plate all nicely dressed. That will never happen. Not a single problem of the class struggle has ever been solved in history except by violence.**
>
> **99** Vladimir Lenin, 1918

> **All those who do not follow the line which I have laid down will be broken.**
>
> **99** Ho Chi Minh, leader of Vietnamese Communists, 1946.

> **Man becomes hardly more, in Communism, than a depersonalised cog in the turning wheel of the state.**
>
> **99** Martin Luther King, Civil rights leader, 1958.